DUI SURVIVAL GUIDE

FOR GOOD PEOPLE WHO MADE

SIMPLE MISTAKES

Jonathan Dichter, Esq.

Founding Attorney

Dichter Law Office, PLLC
3400 188th St. SW #420
Lynnwood, WA 98037
425-424-9401

Ordering Information:

Quantity sales. Special discounts are available on quantity purchases by corporations, associations, and others. For details, contact the publisher at the address above.

Orders by U.S. trade bookstores and wholesalers. Please contact Dichter Law Office, PLLC - 425-424-9401 - www.DUIHeroes.com.

Printed in the United States of America.

Published in 2024

ISBN: 978-1-7321321-9-1

PREFACE

Being arrested for DUI can be an embarrassing and frightening thing. Your license and liberty are both in jeopardy. The process involves the courts, the police, the Department of Licensing, probation, evaluations, interlocks, and more. It is a daunting experience for someone to go through alone. The stress and fear you may experience can be unrelenting and traumatic.

Fortunately, you don't have to go through it alone. This book will serve as your quick reference guide to working through the process side by side with your attorney's office. It will be a place to gain information, find new questions to ask, and feel comforted by the knowledge that you at least understand the process.

Understanding the process is critical. It demystifies it and allows you to work through it logically and professionally. Doing this with the skill and guidance of your attorney's office will help you navigate the system and come out on the other side (hopefully) with a minimal amount of damage to your world.

I am pleased to say that in this new 2024 edition of the DUI Survival Guide, we have a guest chapter author, Attorney Marisa Feil of FWCanada. Marisa is a Canadian attorney who focuses on questions of entry across the Canadian border, and is a frequent referral for our clients who have questions about entry into Canada. She has written chapter 15 entirely about these issues for us, and we are grateful for her expertise.

DEDICATION

For Elizabeth and Alex.

For our clients.

For the team.

ACKNOWLEDGEMENTS

This book would not have been possible without the support and help of the entire team of dedicated DUIHeroes at Dichter Law Office, who I thank from the bottom of my heart. You guys are the best team I could have possibly assembled to do this work for our clients. Keep it up.

ALSO BY JONATHAN DICHTER

Innovative DUI Trial Tools, 6th Ed., 5th Ed., 4th Ed.

DUI Survival Guide (2018, 2019, 2020, 2021, 2022, 2023)

DISCLAIMER

This publication is intended to be used for educational purposes only. No legal advice is being given, and no attorney-client relationship is intended to be created by reading this material. The author assumes no liability for any errors or omissions or for how this book or its contents are used or interpreted or for any consequences resulting directly or indirectly from the use of this book. For legal or any other advice, please consult an experienced attorney or the appropriate expert who is aware of the specific facts of your case and is knowledgeable of the law in your jurisdiction.

Dichter Law Office, PLLC d/b/a DUIHeroes
3400 188th St. SW
Suite 420
Lynnwood, WA 98037
www.DUIHeroes.com
(425) 424-9401

TESTIMONIALS

"I just wanted to pass along my most sincere appreciation for handling my case and getting my life back on the right track. Even through my most recent missteps, you and the Dichter Law Office have provided exceptional service and support. Absolute certainty is not a feeling that comes easily for me, but I am absolutely certain the results of my litigation would have been dramatically different and far less favorable had I not asked for your help in late March of last year. I will do my best to stay on the path you have so clearly paved for me - one for which I am extremely grateful. I was happy to leave a review of my experience on AVVO today, so I hope it reflects the legal course you've guided me through in the past ten months."

P.R.

****

"I call him my hero. Without them I wouldn't have gotten through this."

N.R.

"DUI? Jonathan is your guy. I could write a lot trying to convince you of this, as my experience with Jonathan was exceptional, but I will just share one telling anecdote. My case went to trial, and it was actually fun watching Jonathan run circles around the prosecutor. When the trial was over, our judge (a man on the bench for 26 years) told me I had chosen an excellent attorney. I couldn't agree more!"

Matt H.

****

"Jonathan was always patient and always available to answer our many questions in detail and in an understandable fashion. He displayed superior intelligence and creativity to ensure that my daughter's case ended with the best possible outcome. I highly recommend Jonathan Dichter without reservation."

Linda

"Jonathan, thank you so much for the time and effort you put into helping me with my case. I have tried to put everything behind me and move on to positive changes. Your kindness and patience with me are very appreciated."

WA

"To be honest, I can't even explain how amazing of a lawyer Jonathan is. I got to listen to him defend me in my DOL hearing and all I can say is WOW. He knows all his laws and rules and he knows how to use them. If you get charged with a DUI, don't even hesitate to call Jonathan. He kept my license from being suspended and because he won my DOL hearing, the court threw out my DUI. He does not waste your time and leaves no stone left unturned. Hands down, he is the best at what he does!"

Nicole O.

"Jonathan shared with me one of his killer strategies to employ in a very difficult DUI case I tried in Kansas City recently. The court reporter said it was the worst video she has ever seen. Still, the jury came back not guilty. And why? Strictly because of Jonathan's strategy that I borrowed. It was genius. If he can help a fellow lawyer, I'm sure he can help you."

Chris A.

TABLE OF CONTENTS

ABOUT THE AUTHOR

Jonathan Dichter is a Washington DUI Defense specialist who has been successfully representing hundreds of clients through DUI and other related criminal offenses since 2004. DUIHeroes is one of the highest rated, most respected DUI specialty firms in the state - thousands of clients have trusted their cases and futures to his DUIHeroes. Jonathan routinely teaches other attorneys his trial skills and DUI strategies, and has a soft spot in his heart for the telling of his client's stories to prosecutors, judges, and juries alike. Jonathan believes that storytelling is a skill that most attorneys lack, and yet is one of the most important tools in his firm's arsenal. With twenty years of experience, Jonathan has become a leading DUI defense specialist in Washington, garnering reductions, not guilty verdicts, and dismissals for many of his clients.

DUIHeroes is a firm built on a team-based, client-centric message. Every client who works with Jonathan and his team of DUIHeroes is treated like family, and their stories are compassionately and respectfully handled to try to get them the best possible results amidst the unrelenting traumatic stress of being charged with a crime like DUI. Jonathan has a bachelor's degree from the University of Akron and graduated from Seattle University School of Law, with honors. He believes there is no case that can't be improved by skilled compassionate counsel. Every one of the DUIHeroes works to ensure his clients are cared for and represented with excellence and empathy. Jonathan's enthusiasm for technology and cutting edge practice means he's available to his clients 24 hours a day and always has their files at his fingertips.

What Sets Jonathan Apart For DUI Defense:

- Nationally Published Author of *Innovative DUI Trial Tools,* 6th Ed.; 5th Ed.; 4th Ed.

- 10.0 Rating on Avvo since 2009

- DUI Super Lawyer - Washington Super Lawyers Magazine 2023 (Rising Star 2014-2018)

- Qualified Standardized Field Sobriety Test Instructor

- Advanced Roadside Impaired Driving Enforcement Qualified

- National Highway Traffic Safety Association DUI Detection Qualified

- Forensic Sobriety Assessment Certified

- Member of the National College for DUI Defense (NCDD)

- Faculty member (NCDD)

- Continuing Legal Education Teacher

- Author of Defense Related Articles

- Unique team based approach to every case

DUIHeroes Handles Cases In:

- Snohomish, King, Skagit, Whatcom Counties, Washington

- Most other cities and counties in Washington State

CHAPTER 1

JONATHAN DICHTER'S EXPERIENCE IN HANDLING DUI CASES

I began my career as a public defense attorney working for a couple of small municipalities. I was practicing municipal public defense, which included all sorts of low-level charges, including DUIs. After that, I began working for another public defense firm in misdemeanor practice, and handled many DUI cases in the surrounding cities. Once I was hired by a private firm, I quickly became the head of their criminal division and focused on DUIs, domestic violence, and misdemeanor cases. Since DUI cases were so common at this firm, I had to learn a lot and become very proficient at handling them. I joined the National College for DUI Defense and the DUI Defense Lawyers' Association, and am a member of the faculty of the National College for DUI Defense.

When I opened my own firm in August, 2009, I continued to focus on DUI and domestic violence cases. Over the course of the following few years, I decided to jettison the rest of my practice and handle DUIs exclusively, as that's what people primarily hired me to do. I began teaching classes for DUIs and writing articles for DUI defense attorneys, focusing primarily on trial strategy. I've taken the National Highway and Traffic Safety Administration's course entitled DUI Detection & Standardized Field Sobriety Testing, which is the basic course that all officers must complete in order to investigate DUI cases. The course requires 24 hours of curriculum-based work, including a full "wet lab" where volunteers are dosed with alcohol in order for trainees to evaluate their performance on field sobriety tests. Ultimately, the trainees must decide whether or not to arrest the person.

Having successfully completed this course, I decided to take an extra step and enroll in a class called Advanced Roadside Impaired Driver Enforcement (ARIDE). Not every law enforcement officer and very few attorneys have taken this class, which can be described as a course that bridges the gap between the sobriety testing program and the drug recognition expert (DRE) program. In other words, it serves a precursor to DRE schooling. It acts a a refresher for the basic course and an introduction to the seven major drug categories and how they affect drivers. I became a qualified instructor of the National Highway and Traffic Safety Administration's DUI Detection and Field Sobriety Testing course. I am qualified to teach this course to lawyers, judges, and investigators, and have done so. In addition, I regularly attend continuing legal education seminars and DUI-specific seminars. I also teach at some of these seminars and have developed a seminar revolving around storytelling as a trial skill, which has been presented both in person as well as virtually to hundreds of DUI lawyers around the country. I am now a nationally recognized innovator in DUI Defense, as the author of the *Innovative DUI Trial Tools* (now in its 6th Edition), published by James Publishing.

Over the past decade, my office has become increasingly sought after to consult with attorneys on their DUI cases and provide advice about how to defend their clients. For five years, I served as a member of the board of governors for the Washington Association for Criminal Defense Lawyers. In addition, I've been on the Washington Super Lawyers Magazine's DUI rising stars list from 2014-2018, which is something that fewer than three percent of all attorneys can say. Last year I was named to the Washington Super Lawyers DUI Super Lawyers list.

CHAPTER 2

HOW ARE DUI CHARGES DEFINED IN WASHINGTON?

By definition, a DUI in Washington results from driving a motor vehicle while one's ability to drive is affected to any appreciable degree by drugs or alcohol. You'll notice that there's no numbers in that statement. There is no "legal limit," as some people call it in Washington State. There is however, an "illegal limit." Affected driving is a very subjective term, and the legislature needed a way to evaluate what being "affected"

by a substance really meant. In their infinite wisdom, they eventually decided to set a per se limit, which is a blood (or breath) alcohol concentration (BAC) of 0.08. Using per se limits is a way to eliminate some of that subjectivity inherent in determining the degree to which a person is affected by a substance. This means that regardless of whether someone was actually affected by alcohol, they would be deemed affected by it for legal purposes if they have a BAC of 0.08 or higher.

In other words, a person would be considered to be affected by alcohol as a matter of law. Many states will consider a person to have been affected by alcohol at the time of driving if that person has a BAC of 0.08 or higher. Washington, however, considers a driver affected if their BAC is 0.08 or higher within two hours of driving - not necessarily just at the time of the driving.

Washington became one of the first states in the country to decriminalize the possession and consumption of marijuana, however driving under the influence of marijuana has always been and continues to be illegal. In order for marijuana to be decriminalized, there had to be a per se limit set for it. In Washington, the limit for marijuana is five nanograms of THC per liter of whole blood. A person's ability to drive will be considered "affected" by the substance of marijuana if they are at or above the per se limit of five nanograms of THC within two hours of driving.

Training And Qualifications Needed For Attorneys Who Practice DUI Defense

While additional trainings and qualifications are extremely helpful for attorneys who practice DUI defense, they are not required. In fact, very few DUI attorneys take the time and effort to participate in additional trainings and earn additional qualifications. As far as I know, there are only a small handful of lawyers in this state who have successfully been through all of the courses that I have mentioned. Only the best of the best DUI attorneys will go through these courses, but they are necessary in order to be successful at a high level.

In my opinion, DUI law is one of the most complicated areas of criminal law because DUI cases touch on so many different aspects of criminal law, such as the rules of the road and of operating vehicles, searches and seizures, the gathering of evidence, forensics, and more. This is even more important as a DUI trial attorney, as in my experience, juries are more prejudiced against DUI defendants than any other defendant in the criminal justice system.

CHAPTER 3

MISCONCEPTIONS PEOPLE HAVE ABOUT A DUI ARREST

The biggest misconception that people have about being arrested for a DUI is that they cannot be charged with a DUI if their BAC was below 0.08. Since a person can still be affected by alcohol while having a BAC below 0.08, a person can still be charged with a DUI. Moreover, the state can utilize an expert witness who can present a retrograde extrapolation (which is a scientific way to try to work backwards from a breath or blood test number over time and in order to show what a person's alcohol level was at the time that they were driving). For example, if someone had a BAC of 0.07 two hours after having driven, then that expert witness would attempt to show that their BAC must have been higher than 0.07 when they were actually driving.

Another misconception that people have is that just because they weren't taken to jail or given a "citation" that they were never actually arrested for DUI. However, a person does not have to be taken to jail in order to be arrested, and just because a person wasn't booked into jail doesn't mean that they weren't arrested. If an individual was offered or agreed to take a formal breath test, or had their blood drawn for testing at some time, then they must have been arrested for DUI. If someone was arrested for DUI and was not booked into jail, then it was probably their first offense. In fact, it is very common for the police to not book someone on a first offense. However, it is mandatory under Washington Law that someone with prior offenses be booked into the jail until they see a Judge. The prosecutor's office actually has two years to file charges on a basic DUI. There are individuals who will think they were never arrested or charged and yet get a court date out of the blue 18 months later. This has been especially true during the budget cuts, economic turmoil, and shutdowns of the COVID-19 era, as prosecutors backlogs have become increasingly massive. In some counties we have even seen cases filed at or slightly **beyond** the statute of limitations, which can (in some circumstances) lead to dismissal of cases.

A third misconception that many people have is the belief that if they had a BAC of 0.08 (or higher), then there is no way that a lawyer would be able to help them. However, this is not true; 95 percent of my job involves negotiating settlements and penalties, and lowering offenses. In fact, I have rarely (if ever) encountered a case in which there was nothing I could do to try to help. It is important to consider a case from all angles and ensure that it is evaluated thoroughly.

There is also a lot of misunderstanding that surrounds giving consent versus refusing blood or breath testing. Washington is a presumed breath test or implied consent state, which means that by simply having a driver's license, a person implicitly consents to a breath test if an officer has a probable cause to believe that they are driving while under the influence. A breath test will be offered, and a person does not have the right to demand a blood test. In certain situations, such as refusals and more serious cases, Officers can choose to get a signed subpoena from a judge authorizing a blood test, and officers are more frequently employing this tactic. Sadly, this can further delay filing of a case, as the toxicology lab is taking nearly one year or more to return blood samples to law enforcement at the time of this writing.

CHAPTER 4

MISTAKES THAT PEOPLE MAKE AFTER A DUI ARREST

There are several common mistakes that people make after being arrested for a DUI, but there are also several common mistakes that people make during an initial stop **before** being arrested for DUI. Despite the fact that everyone has a right to remain silent, very few people actually do. If someone wants to help their defense attorney with their DUI case, the best thing they can do is avoid talking to the officer more than is necessary.

When people begin to talk, they give officers additional information and offer to do voluntary tests, which makes their cases significantly more difficult to defend. The next best step a person can take is to hire and consult with a specialized DUI attorney, and **fast**!

There are a couple of different ways in which a person can sabotage their case before even speaking with an attorney. When a person has a BAC of 0.08 or above, or refuses to take the breath test altogether, they will end up with an administrative sanction from the Washington State Department of Licensing, which we typically refer to as a Department of Licensing (DOL) hearing. DOL hearings are routinely the worst part of the process for people, and statistically most people will lose. With that said, there are ways that a person can maximize their chances of winning.

Your timeline is only SEVEN days - this is why you have to act fast! You have one week to request a hearing and your license could be suspended in as soon as 30 days! Your attorney should give you appropriate advice on how and when to mail your request.

One of the biggest mistakes people make is simply not taking advantage of the DOL hearing. Some people might miss the seven day window or not want to pay the $375 fee associated with scheduling it, but the hearing is one of the most important parts of the process in terms of accomplishing a client's goals. Most often, I will subpoena the officer to that hearing and have unfettered access to him without a prosecutor there to shut me up. DOL hearings give me the benefit of being able to craft a defense before the court process even gets started. This can be crucial, especially when many of the largest counties in Washington State are months (or in some cases years) behind on their filings, meaning it could be half a year or more before you see the inside of a courthouse. The DOL process is often over by then! When clients decide to skip the DOL hearing, they effectively cut off a huge part of my skillset in that regard and eliminate one of the most important aspects of the process. In short: **win, lose or draw - always request a DOL hearing.**

Another common mistake that people make is hiring the wrong lawyer to get started on their case. If someone hires an attorney who doesn't know what they are doing, it could seriously harm their case. It's important to find the best attorney possible and follow their instructions. (For tips on how to find the best attorney, see the last chapter in this book, or the DUI Q&A series on our YouTube channel @DUIHeroes)

Trying to figure it out on their own or getting bad advice is another very common mistake that people make. Sometimes people contact me once they are already halfway through their case, and while it would have been more beneficial for me to have been involved from the start, I may be able to undo some of the damage.

In defending a DUI case, most (if not all) of my clients will be asked to get an alcohol and drug evaluation to determine whether or not there's a significant problem with alcohol or drugs and whether treatment is needed. Most clients come to me with some knowledge of this process, having heard about it or read about it online. Some people get really worried about the alcohol and drug evaluation and try to complete it in advance, and they may even have an interlock device installed in their car before it's required.

Taking these sorts of steps in advance could end up being needless, or they may be done incorrectly. I always tell people that their very first step should be to find the right lawyer and go about things one step at a time - most lawyers will in fact have their own process they want you to follow. In theory, a person may be able to gather enough information from the internet and other resources in order to properly deal with a DUI, but they shouldn't go about it that way - just like you could conceivably learn how to take out your own appendix online, but a skilled and trained surgeon is probably a better bet.

CHAPTER 5

PULLED OVER FOR A DUI?

In order for a person to be pulled over on suspicion of DUI in Washington, the officer generally needs to have reasonable suspicion of a traffic infraction (speeding, swerving, crossing a lane line, or being involved in an accident). More often than not, people will be initially stopped by police officers for something like those infractions (or even something far more innocuous like expired tabs) and the officer will then see or smell something that leads them to believe they have been consuming a substance like alcohol.

Although the same is true for drugs, officers are primarily trained to detect intoxication by alcohol. In fact, the vast majority of DUI cases involve alcohol as opposed to drugs.

An officer might notice that a person has bloodshot eyes, slurred speech, or difficulty retrieving their driver's license before asking the person whether or not they have been drinking or how much they have had to drink. At that point, it would be safe to assume that the officer plans on investigating for DUI.

For the most part, DUIs in Washington are gross misdemeanors punishable by up to a year in county jail and a $5000 fine. There are circumstances that will make a DUI a felony, such as at least three prior offenses, or bodily harm inflicted upon another person.

Most of our clients are very honest people, but a lot will try to minimize or talk their way out of a DUI. For example, a person might say that they've just had a "couple of drinks," and an officer will usually request that the person submit to standardized field sobriety tests so that they can confirm that the person is okay to drive. An officer may ask the person to step out of their car in order to isolate the smell of alcohol from any other passengers in the vehicle. Depending on a person's performance on the standardized field sobriety tests, the officer may be able to arrest them for DUI.

Roadside Breath Tests And Standardized Field Sobriety Tests

Standardized field sobriety tests were created and later scientifically studied and validated by the National Highway and Traffic Safety Administration and the International Association of Chiefs of Police. A list of field sobriety tests was studied extensively for decades and was boiled down to just three: the horizontal gaze nystagmus test, the walk and turn test, and the one leg stand test. These tests are the same regardless of where in the country someone is located.

The horizontal gaze nystagums (HGN) test is a test where the officer will move a stimulus (usually a finger or a pen) across your field of vision several times looking for an involuntary jerking of your eyeball as you gaze to the side. When you have a central nervous system depressant (like alcohol) in your system, the muscles around your eyes will be affected by it without your knowledge or control. The officer will be able to detect this.

The walk and turn test is a physical test where the officer will instruct you to walk nine steps heel-to-toe up a line, turn around, and walk nine steps heel-to-toe back down the line. When you have a central nervous system depressant in your system your ability to balance and coordinate your movements is limited, and the officer will also be able to detect this.

The one leg stand test is a physical test where the officer will instruct you to stand on one leg for a period of time, counting as you look at it. Just like the walk and turn test, the officer will be able to detect problems in your ability to balance and coordinate your movements.

To be clear, these tests are in no way perfect. In fact, they're riddled with problems and if they're not performed exactly as they're supposed to be, the conclusions that the officer can draw from them are severely limited.

Non-standardized field sobriety tests have not been studied in a particular way and do not come with a standardized set of instructions or method of grading. These tests include the finger to nose test, the finger dexterity test, saying the alphabet, and the Romberg balance test, among others. Since these tests are non-standardized, scientific conclusions cannot be drawn from them. However, they can nevertheless be administered for observational purposes. For example, if someone has difficulty saying the alphabet or counting backwards from 53 to 38, then the officer would be able to make note of that observation, but would not be able to say that they believe that person's ability to drive was impaired based on those observations. If done correctly, poor performance on standardized field sobriety tests allow an officer to draw conclusions regarding a person's ability to safely operate a vehicle.

In Washington, field sobriety tests are completely voluntary, and a person **should** not be penalized in any way for not doing them. However, there is some recent Washington state case law that suggests that not consenting to the field sobriety tests could be used against a person in court as consciousness of guilt. In other words, it might be argued that the reason a person refused the field sobriety tests is because they knew that they were indeed intoxicated and did not want to perform poorly on them.

The general wisdom is that voluntary tests such as these shouldn't be performed when offered, but as always, getting legal advice in the moment you are being offered them is your best course of action. Put simply: **when in doubt, call a lawyer.**

CHAPTER 6

AM I REQUIRED TO TAKE A BREATH TEST AT THE POLICE STATION?

A person is not required to take the breath test that is administered at the police station. However, there is an implied consent statute in Washington stating that a person has agreed with the Department of Licensing to consent to a breath test if one is requested by an officer. A person retains the right to refuse the breath test, but they will lose their driver's license for a minimum of one year (possibly longer if convicted in criminal court).

In addition, a person can expect to lose their license for no fewer than 90 days if they consent to a blood or breath test and have a BAC of 0.08.

The breath testing device in Washington State is manufactured by a German company, and is called the Draeger Alcotest 9510. Many people refer to what's called a "Breathalyzer," which is a brand name of a particular type of breath testing machine and isn't actually used in Washington State (think "Kleenex" vs. tissue). It is designed to read a breath sample using both infrared and electrochemical technology. This "new machine" is supposedly better than the old DataMaster Washington used, but it has just as many problems. In fact, in late 2019, the Draeger Alcotest 9510 was the subject of a New York Times Investigative exposè entitled *These Machines Can Put You In Jail, Don't Trust Them.* Moreover, in 2021, the Washington State Patrol admitted to the Washington Association of Prosecuting Attorneys that the Draeger Alcotest 9510 had **not followed the laws** regarding how it is to measure breath samples since the inception of the program. After nearly a year of litigation, the Washington Administrative Code was updated to reflect the truth as to how the machine calculates the breath samples, but not before our State Toxicologist (Dr. Fiona Couper) was found to have given false and misleading testimony in thousands of cases.

Whether or not someone should consent to a breath test is hard to say, and the best advice I could give would be for them to speak to a lawyer as soon as possible upon their arrest.

What Happens After I Am Booked Into Custody?

Most people who receive first-time DUIs do not get booked into custody, but instead tested and released from custody.

In late 2019 a law known as Hailey's Law in Washington was struck down by the Washington State Supreme Court. As a result officers are no longer required to impound the vehicles of people arrested for DUI.

When an individual is released from custody after a DUI arrest, they will usually be given a copy of their breath test results and a copy of the request for a DOL hearing. Very rarely will a person be given a citation or court date. While only some people get booked into jail after a first offense, it is required that a person be booked on a second or subsequent offense. However, it is absolutely a bondable offense (meaning the judge will set bail and you can post money to get out of jail) once that person sees a judge, which usually happens within 24 to 72 hours. If a person is booked on a misdemeanor charge in Washington, then it is a requirement that bail be set.

If a person is convicted of DUI in Washington, then they will face mandatory minimum penalties based on the results of their breath or blood test and the number of prior offenses they received in the preceding seven years (10 for felony calculations). Prior offenses include DUIs that were amended, as well as charges that were dismissed through the deferred prosecution program. Some people will assume that if they received a DUI ten years prior, then it won't affect them. However, that is not the case; it may not count for the mandatory minimum purposes, but judges and prosecutors will still be aware of it, and can make decisions based on it.

Moreover, when someone is released from custody or arraigned at a later date in court, they will be under the jurisdiction of the court. This means that the court can impose reasonable conditions on their behavior, such as avoiding trouble, not driving until their ride has been insured, avoiding the consumption of alcohol, and consenting to any breath or blood test requested. There is also a requirement that anyone with a prior DUI from any time in history who has a new alcohol related DUI case pending must either be subjected to a 24/7 alcohol monitoring program, or have an ignition interlock device installed in their vehicle for the duration of the case. This means that if someone has a prior offense, then they will be driving with an ignition interlock device (or wearing an ankle bracelet continuously monitoring their blood for alcohol consumption) within five days of the date of their arraignment.

Are There Any Exceptions To Mandatory Interlock Provisions on Alcohol DUIs for Repeat Offenders In Washington?

Unfortunately, there are no exceptions to the mandatory Interlock requirement for repeat alcohol offenders in Washington; if someone is not driving, then the court will be required to impose a 24/7 alcohol monitoring program. In some cases, the court has allowed people to sign a declaration of non-driving, which is a promise to avoid driving until the court grants them permission. However, some courts do not have the ability to allow people to sign a declaration of non-driving. Some courts do allow for a work vehicle exception as well. The best course of action is to consult with a lawyer about your particular needs and worries.

CHAPTER 7

FIRST APPEARANCE IN COURT AFTER A DUI ARREST

The time when a person will be required to make a first appearance in court after a DUI arrest will depend on where and how that person received the DUI. I frequently work in the King County District Court and Snohomish County District Court, both of which have large prosecutor's offices, huge filing loads, and are backlogged on their appearances. For example, if someone were to be pulled over by Washington State Patrol today, then they might have their first appearance at some point within the next six to even twelve months **or more**! However, the municipal courts tend to work a lot faster, which means a person could have an arraignment within days of their arrest.

"Appearance" is a term that requires definition and discussion at this point. The COVID-19 era has shown the court system that many of the hearings we've come to accept as routine are either unnecessary or unnecessary to do in person. As such, the Washington State Supreme Court has created a new court rule as of 2021 regarding the presence of a defendant in court.

This new rule authorizes remote (or virtual) appearances at arraignment, trial and sentencing. The remarkable thing about this new rule is that it also removes the requirement of the defendant to be present at most other hearings unless the court has a specific reason to order the appearance of the defendant. Your lawyer may be able to appear on your behalf, saving you time away from work and your family. This rule has varied in application from court to court, and many courts are now again requiring in person appearances for some hearings, such as arraignments. For the most up to date information about your court appearance, ask your attorney for assistance.

What Happens To My Driver's License After I Have Been Charged With A DUI?

The police are not allowed to confiscate or punch a hole in a person's driver's license anymore when they arrest them for a DUI. In terms of a person's driving privileges or license to drive within the state, their license will be up for grabs in two different ways. If someone has a blood alcohol concentration of 0.08 or above, or if they refuse to give a breath test, then they will have an administrative hearing through the Department of Licensing, which will occur by telephone. The administrative hearing examiner is considered the "judge," but they are not independent administrative law judges as they are in most other states. Instead, they are employees of the Washington State Department of Licensing, and their job is to uphold suspensions. Statewide, the average win rate on these administrative hearings is less than 20 percent, meaning that about 80 percent of people will lose their license administratively.

Our DUIHeroes win about 40 percent of the time[1], but it is important to understand that even if someone wins the administrative hearing, it doesn't mean that they will be able to keep their license. This is because if they are later convicted in court, then mandatory minimum penalties will be imposed, one of which can be license suspension. Suspensions may be for as few as 90 days, or for as long as four years, depending on your criminal history. In addition, anyone who is convicted of DUI will be required to have an ignition interlock device in their vehicle for anywhere from one to 10 years. If the DUI gets reduced to something like reckless driving, then there will be a mandatory 30-day license suspension (and occasionally in certain circumstances, up to a six month interlock requirement afterwards).

While all of this sounds like incredibly bad news, a couple of years ago the legislature did

---

[1] Every case is different, and this numbers is an approximation only.

something really nice for our clients by creating what's called the ignition interlock license. An ignition interlock license is a temporary driver's license that everyone is eligible for during a required suspension period. It is not a work or school permit, and is not limited to certain locations or times of the day; it is a full-fledged license to drive wherever a person needs to go (within the State). With that said, it does require that the driver have a high-risk type of insurance called SR-22 insurance and a functioning ignition interlock device in their car (although there is a work vehicle exemption to the interlock requirement).

To put it simply, if someone was legally able to drive before receiving a DUI, then there should never be a day that they cannot legally drive after receiving that DUI. Recently, the DOL created a new streamlined system for requesting these licenses. It is highly likely you'll need an account online with License eXpress through the DOL. Consult your attorney for more details and information, as well as assistance in getting this set up.

CHAPTER 8

SENTENCES FOR A DUI CONVICTION

The typical sentences for a DUI conviction in Washington are divided into two categories: low-level mandatory minimum penalties and high-level mandatory minimum penalties. DUI convictions involving a blood alcohol concentration of 0.15 or lower, or the involvement of non-alcohol related substances such as marijuana or prescription drugs, would fall into the low-level category. The only time that a DUI will land in the higher category is when there was a BAC above 0.15 or a refusal of a test. The mandatory minimum penalty on a low-level first offense is 24 consecutive hours in jail or 15 days of in-home monitoring. The mandatory minimum fine is $990.50. The mandatory minimum driver's license suspension is for 90 days, and the mandatory minimum interlock is for one year. A convicted person will have a mandatory alcohol and drug evaluation, and mandatory treatment if it is deemed necessary. A person will also be on probation for a maximum of five years.

High-level mandatory minimum penalties on a first offense involving a BAC of 0.15 or higher include two days in jail or 30 days of in-home monitoring, and a mandatory minimum fine of $1,245.50. The mandatory minimum driver's license suspension for this category is for one year. If someone refused the breath test, then the suspension would be for two years. A convicted person would be on probation for a maximum of five years.

If the driver had prior offenses, then the mandatory minimums would skyrocket. If someone has a prior offense with a BAC below 0.15, then the mandatory minimum penalty would increase from one day in jail to 30 days in jail followed by 60 days of in-home electronic monitoring. *As of 2022, the alternative sentence of 4 days jail followed by 180 days of electronic monitoring has been **eliminated** by the legislature, and now the court must find a substantial risk to a defendant's physical or mental wellbeing before imposing anything other than the actual mandatory minimum.* The mandatory minimum fine with a prior offense increases to $1,245.50, and there would be a two-year license revocation. A convicted person will have a mandatory drug and alcohol evaluation, and mandatory treatment if it is deemed necessary. A person will also be on probation for five years.

If someone has a prior offense with a BAC above 0.15, then the mandatory minimum penalty would increase from two days in jail to 45 days in jail followed by 90 days of in-home monitoring. *As of 2022, the alternative sentence of 6 days jail followed by 6 months of electronic monitoring has been **eliminated** by the legislature, and now the court must find a substantial risk to a defendant's physical or mental wellbeing before imposing* *anything other than the actual mandatory minimum.* The mandatory minimum fine with a prior offense increases to $1,670.50, and there would be a 900-day license revocation or a three-year revocation if the person refused the test.

If someone has two prior offenses involving a BAC below 0.15, then the mandatory minimum penalty would be 90 days in jail followed by 120 days of in-home monitoring. There would be a fine of $2,095, and a three-year license revocation. The same probationary conditions apply across the board. For a third offense, the mandatory minimum penalty is 120 days in jail followed by 150 days of in-home monitoring. There would be a fine of $2,945.50 and a four-year license revocation. If someone has three prior offenses within a 10-year period, then their fourth offense would be considered a felony. At that point, an individual would be facing prison time. There is a mandatory minimum grid which helps to clarify the differences in penalties for different circumstances.

NEW IN 2024 - REPEAT DUIs AFFECT FIREARM RIGHTS

As of July 23, 2023, a new collateral consequence for DUI convictions if you have a prior offense of any kind became law in Washington. Even if amended or deferred, a second offense DUI in Washington now results in a loss of your right to possess firearms. It will be a separate **felony** criminal offense (Unlawful Possession of a Firearm in the Second Degree) if a person who has lost their firearm rights for these reasons should be found in possession of a firearm. Although the right to possess a firearm may be restored by petitioning a Superior Court, this new loss of Constitutional Rights is a huge consequence for some, and must be considered carefully when handling a second or subsequent DUI charge.

Enhancing Or Aggravating Factors For DUI Charges

There is one main enhancing or aggravating factor for DUI charges in Washington, which is the presence of a passenger under the age of 16 in the vehicle at the time of driving. There are other considerations that the court is supposed to be looking into as potential enhancements, such as the involvement of an accident or wrong-way driving, but it is not required that the court take such details into consideration.

CHAPTER 9

DUI DEFENSE – THE PROCESS

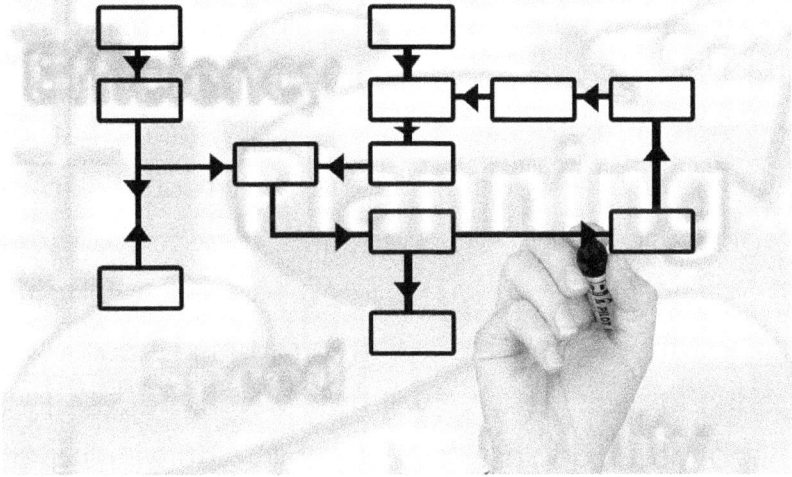

Our firm approaches defending a DUI case in a very methodical way. Over the course of 20 years in practice, I have developed a process that tends to end in better results for our clients. When approaching the defense of a DUI case, the first step involves obtaining copies of the police report and any other discovery. Depending on where the documents and discovery are located, it could take days to weeks to actually obtain them. Next, our attorneys will review the evidence. We will review the police reports and other evidence (radio logs, videos if there are any, for example), and will go out to the scene if needed. Next, we will consider information gained from our clients in a confidential questionnaire. Finally, we will sit down with our clients and discuss the good and bad aspects of their case, as well as determine whether negotiation or litigation is the best route to take. Most cases begin with negotiation, because there is no harm or risk associated with it. Successful negotiation often results in a reduced charge or reduced penalties. We will then weigh the result of negotiation against the possibility of winning at trial.

Using Private Investigators And Experts

Once the initial assessment of a DUI case has been made, we may recommend the use of experts and/or investigators. Whether or not we decide this will depend on whether or not the client wants to go to trial. If the client wants to go to trial, then we may consult with a breath testing expert, blood testing expert, or a professional who reconstructs accidents. However, these are decisions that would generally be made only if a case is heading to trial. Knowing when to use an expert as well as how to use them once they're hired is a critical point in higher end DUI Defense.

Obtaining Discovery And Reviewing It

We try to obtain discovery as quickly as possible in a DUI case. Washington State Patrol put together a discovery website that allows us to retrieve the records and databases from all of the breath testing machines, the training materials for officers, and a resume from every toxicologist and technician involved in the DUI process statewide. This information is available for historical cases as well, free of charge. We often make public records requests to obtain the police reports in advance of the charging decisions. Regardless of when or whom we receive the reports and discovery from, our office will review them immediately. In Washington, a client is also allowed to read the police reports and watch the videos, but in many cases, they cannot be given a copy of either due to court rules.

Does It Help A Case If A Client Can See Discovery And Go Through It With You?

It can be helpful to a case when a client reviews the discovery with me. I have my clients fill out a detailed questionnaire before meeting with them to review discovery. The questionnaire provides me with a lot of information that I may not have gotten from reading the police report. It's important to note that police reports are never written as pure fact, but as persuasive documents by officers who must justify their decision to arrest someone. Clients often have very different viewpoints on what occurred during a DUI arrest. For example, we recently handled a case wherein my client told us that the police report suggested that was a voicemail was left for me by the arresting officer; since I never received a voicemail, I knew that what the officer stated in his report was untrue.

CHAPTER 10

USING STANDARDIZED FIELD SOBRIETY TEST AND BREATH TEST RESULTS IN DUI DEFENSE

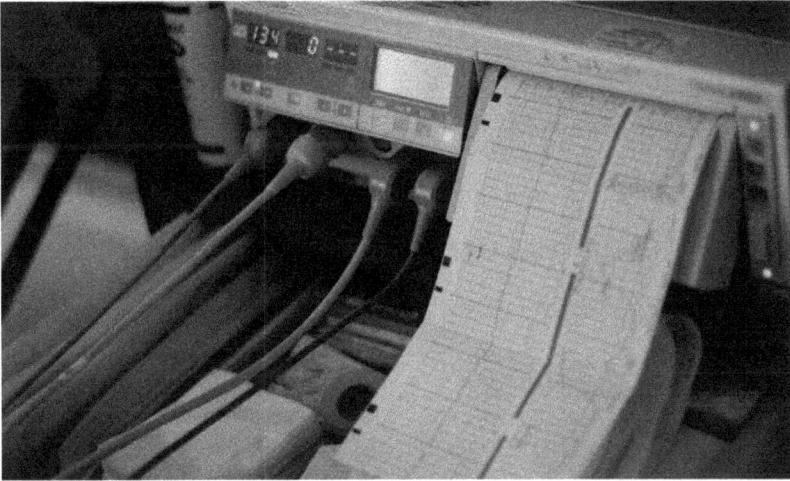

It is difficult to say how standardized field sobriety test results and breath test results are used to defend DUI cases. Washington State Patrol has put together a "check-the-box" sheet for scoring the roadside standardized field sobriety tests. This means that I get a field sobriety test page that shows a client's score. However, this is not helpful to me because I have no way of knowing whether or not the scores are accurate; I don't know what instructions they gave or how the client actually performed. Now that a lot of officers have dash cameras built into their vehicles (and some jurisdictions also wear body worn cameras), we can watch the field sobriety tests and I can listen to the instructions that were given, which can be very helpful. If the instructions were not given correctly, then the field sobriety tests would have been carried out incorrectly (you'll recall that because these tests are standardized they need to be performed in the same way every time), which I could use to defend the case.

In terms of breath test results, I will obtain all of the information from the breath testing machine, including the quality assurance protocol reports, repair reports, and calibration records. I can literally look at the breath test machine with a fine toothed comb in order to seek any possible way in which to challenge it. I can also often request video of the breath testing machine room so we can observe how the test was administered. If needed, there is a pulmonologist we consult with regarding specific scientific questions regarding breath testing and alcohol in the airways.

How Do You Use A Motion To Suppress Evidence In a DUI Case?

A motion to suppress evidence would generally only be used if a DUI case is going to trial. Motions don't occur during negotiation because once we file them, the prosecutor's office generally stops negotiating with us; they have no incentive to negotiate if they think we are going to fight the case in court.

At a motions hearing, we can argue to suppress a variety of things. Some of these considerations include whether or not the officer performed his job correctly and legally, and whether or not the evidence was gathered correctly.

If we can show that an officer made an error, then the evidence (or sometimes the whole case) could potentially be thrown out. If we can show that the initial stop itself was invalid, then the entire case could be thrown out. If the results of a field sobriety or breath test are thrown out, the prosecution could still choose to proceed with the case. However, the prosecution's case would likely be weakened by the absence of breath test results.

In order to explain this, I use a chess analogy, wherein a trial is the chess game; each piece on the board is a piece of evidence that one side or the other has, but a trial is a chess game that is already in progress when the parties begin playing; the process of filing motions is the process of deciding which pieces are where, and the process of playing it out is the process of trial.

When Does Sentencing Take Place If Someone Pleads Guilty To A DUI?

In most of the courts in Washington, sentencing takes place at the same time as the plea, and the whole process only takes about 10 minutes. However, some courts have changed the way that sentencing is done, and this can affect my clients. These courts have decided that some clients who receive a DUI (especially if they have a prior offense) must go to the probation department for a pre-sentencing interview. The sentencing hearing is set to take place about 30 or 45 days after the plea hearing. Most first time offenders in Snohomish County are sentenced at the time of their plea.

CHAPTER 11

FACTORS THAT CAN HELP MITIGATE A DUI SENTENCE

The fact that a judge can't go below the mandatory minimum penalties in a DUI case makes mitigating sentences for DUI tricky, which is why we always try to negotiate to lower offenses that don't have mandatory minimum penalties. In the worst case scenario, a client will end up with a DUI conviction and will face the mandatory minimum penalties, but we can work to mitigate the damage by ensuring that the client has completed the drug and alcohol evaluation and class work. The more that a client can do in advance, the better off they will be when it comes time for sentencing.

Sometimes a person will be switched to a lower level of probation, which might be less expensive in terms of court costs. In other cases, a person may have a few days of jail time taken off of their sentence, if possible. There is always the potential for a judge to make decisions that will benefit an individual, especially if that individual completed everything that was required of them in advance. When a person receives a DUI, the very first thing they should do is hire a lawyer and follow their instructions.

Are There Alternative Programs Available In Washington For First-Time DUI Offenders?

Generally speaking, there are no alternative programs available in Washington for first-time DUI offenders. There is something in Washington called a deferred prosecution, and many clients tell me that they want their DUI "deferred". However, having a first-time DUI deferred would usually be a big mistake. There are three different things that can be deferred in Washington, they all have completely different meanings, and most people drastically misunderstand them.

The first thing that people hear about is what's called a deferred finding, which is available in civil traffic infractions involving traffic tickets. A deferred finding allows a person to have their case dismissed once every seven years upon payment of a fee. However, this is not applicable in criminal cases or criminal DUIs.

A deferred sentence is designed for first-time misdemeanors in Washington, and allows a judge to put someone on probation for a period of time. Once that person finishes their probation, then their case will be dismissed. However, deferred sentences are specifically not available for DUIs.

The only deferred option that applies to DUIs is deferred prosecution, which is designed as a treatment program alternative to prosecution. In order to qualify for deferred prosecution, a person must be diagnosed as an alcohol or drug-dependent individual and be deemed in need of a two-year, extensive treatment program (there is also a mental health option). If a client would rather participate in the treatment program than be punished for a DUI, then the court will allow it, and the individual will be put on probation for five years. During that probationary period, the person would be required to attend two AA meetings per week.

The reason that this is not generally done for first-time DUIs is because most people who have only received one DUI are not alcoholics, but instead simply normal individuals who made an easy to make error in judgment. So, most first-time offenders would not even qualify for this option. In addition, if someone is alcohol-dependent, then they are statistically much more likely to get a second or subsequent DUI over the following seven years, and a person is only eligible for deferred prosecution one time per lifetime. On first-time offenses, it's often a better solution to try to negotiate a better deal or take the case to trial.

CHAPTER 12

HOW OFTEN ARE YOU ABLE TO HAVE DUI CHARGES OR SENTENCES REDUCED?

About 95 percent of first-time DUI cases that my office handles get reduced or dismissed altogether. However, this does not mean that an individual sitting in my office has a 95 percent chance of getting a positive result on their case; it means that in all of the cases that I have handled prior to that moment, about 95 percent ended in positive results for my clients. Approximately 89 or

90 percent of second or subsequent DUI cases get reduced or dismissed completely[2].

What Can I Do To Help Myself Get A Positive Outcome In My DUI Case?

There are five things that a person can do to increase their chances of receiving a positive outcome in their DUI case.

First, a person can do what their attorney asks them to do in a timely fashion. This means that if the attorney asks someone to get an alcohol and drug evaluation at a particular agency, they shouldn't wait to do so until the day before court. If a person doesn't understand what their attorney is telling them, they should ask questions for clarification. Often, your attorney can help you set up the appointment, or even make it for you.

Secondly, a person should always be open, honest, truthful, and forthcoming with their attorney. Attorney-client confidentiality means

---

[2] Every case is different, and prior case results can not in any way predict future case results. These numbers are approximations that were accurate based on years of data at the time of writing.

that an attorney cannot disclose the information that their client gives to them, but if a client lies to their attorney, then that attorney could make a mistake on the record, which would reflect poorly on the attorney and their client. It is also important that a client avoids telling their attorney about anything which the attorney did not ask. It's not that we don't want to know - but rather that knowing too much could hurt our abilities to defend you. We ask what we need to know.

Thirdly, a person should not hesitate to contact their lawyer if they have a question, concern, or are just worried in general. People should not rely on their friends, relatives, or social media for information; they should speak with the lawyer whom they are paying to represent them.

Fourthly, a person should avoid getting into any additional trouble while their case is pending; don't commit any bank robberies, don't build nuclear weapons, and don't drink and drive. In other words, just stay out of trouble. In fact, it's my preference that my clients avoid the possession or consumption of alcohol and all non-prescribed substances while the case is pending.

Lastly—and this is often the hardest rule—it's important that clients let their attorneys do the worrying; that's the attorney's job, and it's how they make their livelihood. If a client begins to worry about their DUI case, they should call and speak with their attorney.

Does Starting Voluntary Rehab Or Counseling Help My DUI Case Or Not?

Starting voluntary rehab or counseling might not help a DUI case. I have all of my clients undergo an alcohol and drug evaluation, but they shouldn't do so before meeting with me; they should do it in the way and at the location that I tell them to. Rehab programs and AA meetings are rarely needed on a first-time offense, but both may be needed on a second a subsequent offense. The hard and fast rule for clients is to hire a lawyer whom they trust, and to follow their instruction one step at a time; they should not get ahead of themselves or ahead of their lawyers.

It should be noted here that if you are in need of counseling, rehab, or services - you should get them immediately. Our office will happily help you do that. There is, however, a distinction between what you need for your health and what I need for your defense.

CHAPTER 13

THINGS THAT COULD HARM YOUR DUI CASE

There are several things that a person should not do in order to avoid harming their DUI case, such as getting into trouble again, not requesting a hearing with the Department of Licensing, not listening to their lawyer's advice, mouthing off to a judge in court, mouthing off in front of a jury in court, and berating the arresting officer in the courthouse (and yes, every one of these things has happened in the past). People should act professionally, respectfully and follow the advice of their lawyers. Generally speaking, if a person is not specifically asked to speak, then they shouldn't.

Do Most DUI Cases Resolve In Some Sort Of Plea Deal? Why Is It The Best Option For Someone?

In our state, almost all DUI cases resolve through plea negotiation. In my office, the percentage of cases that go to trial is about three percent, which means that 97 percent of our cases resolve through plea negotiations. If I'm able to work out a deal with the prosecutor to have a DUI amended to a misdemeanor and there is no jail recommendation on a first offense, then no one can take that amendment away. Negotiations are the safest route because they put the control in the client's hands instead of in the hands of six strangers on a jury.

Comedian Norm Crosby once said, "Never forget when you go to trial that you are putting your life in the hands of 12 people who weren't smart enough to get out of jury duty." Jurors hate drunk drivers; in fact, I think there are fairer trials for sex criminals than drunk drivers. With that in mind, jury trials on DUIs are risky and best avoided when possible.

CHAPTER 14

WHY IS IT IMPORTANT TO WORK WITH A SPECIALIZED ATTORNEY?

It is important to work with an attorney who specializes in handling DUI cases because DUI convictions have lifelong impacts on a person's family, driver's license, livelihood, and record. If a DUI case is handled incorrectly, it can't be undone and could wind up costing a client $12,000 to $15,000 or more. A person has one chance to be represented by the right attorney and avoid the consequences of a DUI conviction. If a person needs brain surgery, they would likely want to see a surgeon who only practices brain surgery; if it were my brain on the line, that's who I would want.

How Do You Advise Clients Who Want To Plead Guilty To A DUI Charge?

Most judges won't let a person plead guilty to a DUI charge at an arraignment. This is because they will want an attorney to review the case first in order to ensure that the person's rights are protected. A DUI conviction will remain on a person's record for the rest of their life, whereas reckless driving, negligent driving, and reckless endangerment charges can generally be vacated from a person's record after 10 years. DUI convictions also carry mandatory jail time and mandatory licensing consequences. So, simply pleading guilty to get it over with is a lifetime decision and not one that should be taken lightly.

What Sets You And Your Firm Apart In handling DUI Cases In Washington?

Our DUIHeroes are set apart from the rest in handling DUI cases in Washington because that is all we do. The specialized training that we've been through and the process I've created has resulted in very positive outcomes for clients. My firm is also set apart by the fact that we use a team-based approach, meaning that our DUIHeroes look at a case from every angle. Our team currently consists of myself, my three associates (Rachel, Kaia, and Christopher), my legal secretary, my law clerk, and our Director of Operations. Why does that matter? For 20 years I have been a defense attorney, for the last 13 years I've been focusing on DUIs, and for the last eight years I've specialized in nothing but DUI cases.

Prior to bringing Rachel on board as an associate in 2017, she worked as a municipal court prosecutor for seven years, which means that she was prosecuting DUIs. This gives her the advantage of viewing a case the way a prosecutor would.

Prior to adding Kaia to the team in 2022, she was a dedicated defense attorney in private and public practice. She is a tireless advocate and always looks for new ways to attack every case.

Before joining our team in 2024, Christopher was a high level King County felony prosecutor working on very serious cases as well as very serious juvenile prosecutions. Christopher has experience with forensics, science, and high stakes high stress cases and gives him an advantage in every case.

All of our DUIHeroes us work as a team, which means we work every case together, so you can feel confident in the skills of your legal team.

Chapter 15

What About Canada?

Marisa Feil, Senior Attorney FWCanada

1-855-316-3555 | info@fwcanada.com

You may be wondering, why are people with criminal histories, even very minor ones, not allowed to enter Canada?

Immigration, Refugees and Citizenship Canada (IRCC) and Canadian Border Services Agency (CBSA) both place massive importance on ensuring the security of Canada and its citizens.

For this reason, they are determined to deny entrance of any and all persons they feel are likely to commit a crime during their visit to Canada.

When entering Canada, you are required to show your passport and any necessary visas to a border agent at the port of entry through which you are passing. When the border agent scans your passport, they will have access to not only the personal information printed on it, but also your criminal record.

Border agents have access to, through their CPIC databases, the United States National Crime Information Center. State police databases are also accessible to CBSA agents.

Border agents at international airports receive passenger lists and conduct background checks on the names that appear on them. A name on the list that produces a criminal record will be flagged for secondary screening. With these records, border agents will determine a person's admissibility to Canada.

The most accurate and up to date information about criminal inadmissibility can be found in the Immigration and Refugee Protection Act (IRPA), which is the official legislation regarding immigration to Canada. Sections 33-43 of the Act deal exclusively with inadmissibility. The section you'll want to focus on is 36—which dictates criminal inadmissibility. The only way to judge if you are indeed criminally inadmissible to Canada is to first translate your conviction into the language of Canadian criminal law.

Does the offense on your record have a counterpart in Canada? If so, then there is a chance that you are inadmissible to Canada. This concept is known as equivalence.

Offenses like DUI and reckless driving can lead to criminal inadmissibility, as they are recognized as indictable offenses in Canada. For example, if you were convicted of a DUI charge within the past ten years, you would not be able to enter Canada.

There are three pathways available to individuals who wish to enter Canada with a criminal record.

1. Submit a Temporary Resident Permit Application

A temporary resident permit (TRP) can grant temporary access to Canada for people who are currently inadmissible due to their criminal records. A TRP application should only be submitted for significant travel, and can be granted for a duration of up to three years. The duration of the TRP may be extended from inside Canada as well.

A TRP is the right choice if you:

Have been convicted outside of Canada for a criminal offense that, if committed in Canada, is equivalent to an indictable offense punishable by a sentence of less than 10 years.

Have been convicted outside of Canada of a crime that would be equivalent to a hybrid offense punishable by a sentence of less than 10 years. A hybrid offense is one that can be prosecuted in Canada either by summary process or by indictment.

Have been convicted of two or more crimes that, if committed in Canada, would be equivalent to two summary offenses.

At the time of publication, TRP processing times are around **six months**, so plan ahead!

2. Submit a Criminal Rehabilitation Application

Criminal rehabilitation is an application offered to those who are eligible for permanent clearance of a past criminal record once enough time has passed. If an individual receives an approval for criminal rehabilitation to enter Canada, they are no longer considered inadmissible and do not require a TRP for entry. The criminal rehabilitation application is a one-time solution that, unlike a TRP, never requires renewal.

In order to be eligible for criminal rehabilitation you must:

Have committed an act outside of Canada that would constitute an offense under the Canadian Criminal Code;

Have been convicted of, or admitted to, committing the act;

Five (5) years must have passed since the full sentence or sentences were completed. This phase includes jail time, fines, and probation.

At the time of publication, rehabilitation applications take about **one full year**, so getting started early is critical.

3. Get a Legal Opinion Letter

An individual with a criminal record can preemptively avoid being found inadmissible to Canada with a legal opinion letter that is addressed to the judicial authority hearing the case. This letter is a document that is drafted by a Canadian immigration attorney, such as FW Canada. Just because a person has a criminal record in their home country does not guarantee that they are criminally inadmissible to Canada. In the letter, the lawyer draws on relevant sections of Canadian law to explain how the conviction does not have an equivalent crime in Canadian law. This information can help the person decide how to respond to charges of a crime and how different outcomes would affect that person's ability to come to Canada.

Do I need an immigration lawyer if I have a DUI conviction?

Both a Temporary Resident Permit and a Criminal Rehabilitation application can be submitted without legal representation.

However, it is advised that individuals looking to maximize their chances of entry seek the assistance of a professional Canadian immigration lawyer. Temporary Resident Permit and Criminal Rehabilitation applications can be confusing, and are often denied if the applicant fails to fill in the required information or abide by all the regulations. Even sending the application to the incorrect consulate can result in it never being reviewed at all. Canadian immigration lawyers assist the individual in completing and submitting this form, to ensure that it is not automatically denied on a technicality. In addition, the role of a Temporary Resident Permit or Criminal Rehabilitation Application is to argue that the individual needs to enter Canada, and does not pose a risk to Canadians. Therefore, an experienced lawyer can assist in the construction of this argument by advising on relevant evidence to include and supporting the individual's collection of documents.

Please note that only Canadian immigration lawyers are eligible to act as representatives on Temporary Resident Permit and Criminal Rehabilitation Applications, as per the regulations of the Canadian government. This is because it is a complex document that is governed by Canadian immigration law, and therefore requires a lawyer who is trained and certified in a Canadian province to oversee its completion.

As outlined above, a TRP or Criminal Rehabilitation application is approved based on the strength of its argument. The final decision is always left to the discretion of the border agent, and therefore there can be no guarantees with regards to who is and who is not admissible. In general, border agents look at the following conditions:

*the number of offenses on a record

*the ages of the DUI and other offenses

*the circumstances of the DUI and other offenses

*the sentencing for the DUI and other offenses

*the purpose of travel, and the evidence provided.

Based on their assessment of the application, they determine if the potential safety risks of allowing the individual into Canada outweigh the person's need for travel.

If one is refused entry from Canada due to criminal inadmissibility from a past DUI conviction or any other offenses, it is important that they address their inadmissibility before attempting to enter again. This is because immediately trying to enter following a refusal will appear to the border agent as an attempt to deceive the Canadian government. This will result in an automatic denial, as well as a potential ban from entering Canada at all. It is advised that the individual consult a Canadian immigration lawyer before they try to enter again.

If an individual is denied entry to Canada because of their DUI conviction, in many instances the deciding border agent will enter a comment into the Canadian government's database. In this comment, they explain why the individual's need to enter Canada did not outweigh the potential safety risks of that person's entry. Following this process, the individual may request these Case Notes to understand what changes to make to future applications to fully address the agent's concerns.

Please note that even if one's application is denied, they are eligible to apply again. Similarly, if one's TRP application is approved and then expires, that individual may also apply again. There is no limit on TRP applications, however a number of denied TRP applications may reflect poorly on an individual's chance of approval for subsequent applications.

It is advisable to speak to an attorney who focuses on DUIs in your area to assess your options. Many defendants plead guilty to a DUI without consulting a lawyer in order to save money and time. They then find out that they are on probation for five years, which means that they will not be eligible to clear their record for the purposes of coming to Canada for another ten years. It is beneficial for an accused to try and get as short a period of probation as possible because this also minimizes the period of inadmissibility to Canada. The required wait time for eligibility for Criminal Rehabilitation does not start until the very last condition of a sentence is completed, and this includes the probation period.

It is possible to apply for permission to enter Canada at a border crossing or port of entry after a DUI conviction. However, it is important to note that there are different considerations depending on the type of border crossing. Since September 11, 2011, when the Canadian and U.S. governments decided that sharing criminal background information would help border security, Canada has access to the FBI's criminal database, which allows them to access information simply by swiping a traveler's passport.

Due to international security protocols at airports, Canadian airports have significant passenger security measures to ensure the safety of passengers of international air travel. Virtually all Canadian airports that accommodate international flights have border services agents ready to greet passengers. These border services agents also often have access to flight lists with passenger information, which allows them to conduct preliminary background checks before the individual arrives at customs and immigration. Whereas in the past not every individual had his or her passport screened, it is now the exception, not the rule, that a passenger landing at an international airport will not be screened. One of the advantages of flying into Canada is that, generally, the immigration officers stationed at the airports are more senior and knowledgeable about admissibility issues because they are required to process individuals from all over the world with many different types of admissibility issues. An individual who has prepared an application for a TRP for assessment at a Canadian port of entry may consider traveling to a Canadian airport because of this fact.

Whereas in the past, an individual was much more likely to undergo a background check at a Canadian airport, virtually all Canadian land crossings are now equipped with scanners that can retrieve an individual's criminal record by scanning passports. While some travelers prefer to travel by car because, if they are denied entry, they can easily turn around and drive back into the U.S., the same is not true of individuals traveling by bus or rail. Individuals who plan on traveling to Canada by bus or rail must be extremely careful when electing to have a TRP assessed at the border. If individuals are deemed to be inadmissible to Canada, they will be responsible for their own transportation back into the U.S. While it may be tempting to decide to drive to Canada to mitigate the risks of the expenses of having to return to the U.S., chances of success may actually be better at a Canadian airport than at a land crossing.

Canadian cruising destinations are increasing in popularity as people are attracted to sightseeing destinations such as Vancouver, Montreal, Quebec City, and St. John. However, past criminal offenses might result in denied entry. Potential cruisers often overlook this problem by failing to realize its severity, and typically cruise lines do not caution their clients about the possibility of denied entry. There have been various cases where people were denied entry to Canada while on a cruise due to a previous DUI conviction. If a cruise departs from Canada, a person who has a past criminal offense would not be able to board the ship unless he has proper documentation. There are various implications depending upon the port of departure and arrival and the itinerary. If the cruise departs from a Canadian destination, a non-Canadian who is deemed inadmissible would be denied entry into Canada before arriving at the ship, and thus the individual would not be able to board. Cruise lines will not refund an individual for being turned away due to criminal reasons. In the event that the cruise departs from an American port and ends in a Canadian city, the inadmissible cruiser would have to exit the country immediately and take the first available flight out of Canada at his own expense. In addition, the inadmissible cruiser would not be able to disembark at any of the excursion stops.

Due to Covid-19, far fewer people have been applying for permits, so the normal processing time has been cut in half. Faster processing times have allowed more requests to be processed at the consulates. The global pandemic has also affected travel restrictions. As a result, most clients who are eligible for a Temporary Resident Permit also meet the exemptions from travel restrictions due to having family in Canada, traveling for essential business, or working to support the fight against Covid-19.

What Not To Do: An Example

After being previously turned away at the Canadian-U.S. border due to her criminal inadmissibility, Kelly Lynn Whittet, a 43-year-old Oregon woman, hid in the back of her boyfriend's father's van in an attempt to avoid Canadian border officials. Whittet and her boyfriend were traveling to the man's home near St. Catherines, Ontario, where they planned on spending the month together. As her boyfriend drove the van to the Blue Water Bridge, Whittet hid underneath some bags and chairs in the back of the vehicle. Whittet's previous entry refusal was based on her U.S. criminal conviction for domestic assault and contempt of court. It was during this previous attempt to enter Canada that Whittet learned of her inadmissibility and of the subsequent procedures required for her to be admitted into the country--namely, applying for a TRP. Oddly enough, some of the required forms for the TRP application were later found in the van. Border agents felt it necessary to search the vehicle after the boyfriend's answers to their routine questions drew suspicion. The boyfriend originally told the CBSA officers that no one else was in the van, but when an officer noticed movement and asked who else was there, Whittet revealed herself to them. The boyfriend then claimed to not know the woman, but Whittet protested that he was only trying to protect her. The boyfriend is still awaiting trial and was released on bail. Meanwhile, the Oregon woman pled guilty to attempting to evade customs and immigration requirements in a Sarnia courtroom on June 22, 2012. Whittet spent 12 days in jail before being deported back to the United States. After imposing the sentence, Justice Mark Hornblower stated that had Whittet followed the proper procedures, she would have likely been granted entry to Canada. Such a privilege is now unlikely for the American woman.

Getting help

Canada Border Services Agency officers have the authority to determine whether an individual is permitted to enter Canada. If an individual appears at the border with a conviction on his or her record and has not received a positive decision on an application for Criminal Rehabilitation or for a TRP, then the officer may make a determination on the individual's admissibility to Canada. Since these officers are not attorneys, it is often difficult for them to conduct an analysis of the foreign statute under which the individual was convicted and its equivalent offense under the Canadian Criminal Code. For this reason, it is advisable to consult a Canadian immigration attorney who can properly conduct this analysis ahead of time. If the determination is made that the individual is inadmissible to Canada, there are different options available depending on the individual's particular circumstances. An experienced Canadian immigration lawyer can prepare the appropriate application and recommend strategies that will increase the individual's chances of entering Canada successfully. A lawyer may recommend any of the following:

Temporary Resident Permit (TRP): to temporarily overcome inadmissibility when an individual is required to be in Canada quickly, if the individual has not yet undergone Criminal Rehabilitation because he or she is not eligible or the application has not yet been processed;

Criminal Rehabilitation: to permanently remove any criminal inadmissibility issues the individual is facing so that future travel to Canada can be done without applying for permission;

Legal opinion letter: to explain why the individual was never criminally inadmissible to Canada because his or her conviction is not equivalent to any Canadian offense, or because the individual was not convicted of the original charges. These types of letters can also be written to explain deemed rehabilitation, as there is no official immigration application to do so. Lawyers representing U.S. clients who are required to travel to Canada (for family or work reasons) are often asked to prepare a letter explaining the effects of a conviction for a DUI on their client's ability to travel to Canada.

What if I don't drive while I'm in Canada?

In many cases, the individual with a DUI or DWI conviction will not be driving a vehicle during their time in Canada. This may be the case for someone who is flying into the country then relying on taxi services, or accompanying a friend or co-worker who will be driving during the trip. However, this does not have any impact whatsoever on the individual's inadmissibility to Canada. Because the Canadian border agent can never fully guarantee that the traveller will not be driving while in Canada, the agent must proceed as though the traveller has the potential to do so. As a result, the individual may still be deemed inadmissible to Canada at the border. For similar reasons, an individual's promise to abstain from alcohol during their stay holds little weight in the assessment of their admissibility.

Will everyone I'm traveling with find out about my DUI conviction?

It is possible to keep one's criminal history private from fellow travelers when crossing the border. The simplest method is by flying into the country, as typically people pass through customs individually and can therefore have a private conversation with the border agent about their DUI and any other offenses on their record. If one has received prior approval to enter Canada, this process is even more painless. It may be slightly more challenging to avoid disclosing your criminal history when driving across the border. In this case, everyone must submit their passports at once, and the individual faces the risk of the border agent addressing his or her inadmissibility in front of the other passengers. In this case as well, prior approval to enter Canada may lower the risk as the border agent could just waive the car through. If the individual does not have prior approval, they will be sent to secondary screening. The actual screening will be confidential, however it may raise questions from fellow travelers as to why they are being delayed.

It may be helpful to note that formal approval to enter Canada is not solely required for the case of a criminal record. Often Canada will request paperwork for entry for other reasons as well, such as health reasons or a past overstay in Canada. Therefore, informing the border agent of paperwork documenting one's approval to enter Canada does not necessarily mean that the individual has a criminal record.

Unlike other Canadian immigration applications, like study permits and visitor's visas, the government does not facilitate admissibility applications for applicants. They will not typically answer phone inquiries, and the information on their website is incomplete. Due to recent cutbacks, the Canadian consulates no longer offer walk-in service for any type of application. Furthermore, changes to the requirements and processing of these applications occur all the time, so it is important to speak to an expert before attempting to cross the Canadian border with a DUI or any other offense. Please remember that only a Canadian lawyer or certified Canadian immigration consultant can receive payment for assisting/ representing an individual in his or her application. Applicants are required to disclose when they have received assistance with their application, whether or not they paid for assistance. New and updated information is always available at www.duicanadaentry.com.

INDEX

NOTES

THIS PAGE INTENTIONALLY LEFT BLANK

THIS PAGE INTENTIONALLY LEFT BLANK

THIS PAGE INTENTIONALLY LEFT BLANK

THIS PAGE INTENTIONALLY LEFT BLANK

www.ingramcontent.com/pod-product-compliance
Lightning Source LLC
Chambersburg PA
CBHW071453200326
41519CB00019B/5719